D0612933

ELIZABETHAN
WRITERS

Charles Nicholl

NPG

Published in Great Britain by National Portrait Gallery Publications,
National Portrait Gallery, St Martin's Place, London WC2H 0HE

ISBN 1 85514 200 7

A catalogue record for this book is available from the British Library

Series Project Editors: Gillian Forrester and Lucy Clark
Series Picture Researcher: Susie Foster
Series Designer: Karen Osborne
Printed by PJ Reproductions, London

Front cover
William Shakespeare, 1564–1616
Attributed to John Taylor (detail)
Oil on canvas, feigned oval, 55.2 x 43.8 cm
© National Portrait Gallery (1)

For a complete catalogue of current publications,
please write to the address above.

CONTENTS

❦

Martin Droeshout sculpsit London

To the Reader.

This Figure, that thou here feeſt put,
    It was for gentle Shakeſpeare cut;
Wherein the Grauer had a ſtrife
    with Nature, to out-doo the life:
O, could he but haue drawne his wit
    As well in braſſe, as he hath hit
Hisface; the Print would then ſurpaſſe
    All, that was euer writ in braſſe.
But, ſince he cannot, Reader, looke
    Not on his Picture, but his Booke.

                                        B. I.

INTRODUCTION

❧

'Reader,' says Ben Jonson curtly, 'looke Not on his Picture, but his Booke.' He is right, of course. The 'booke' he is referring to is the First Folio of Shakespeare's plays, and the picture is the rather bland engraving of the author by Martin Droeshout which forms its frontispiece. But even so, the picture holds our attention. We do not stop looking on it. It is little more than an incised sketch, a naive kind of icon, but somewhere behind that familiar mask – the stiff collar, the domed head, the perfunctory beard – is the face of Shakespeare.

Fortunately, other portraits in the gallery of Elizabethan writers displayed in this book tell us more than this notoriously reticent picture of Shakespeare (and fortunately we know at least one other, more compelling portrait of him). These pictures are not often intimate – the overall style is formal – but they are full of physical presence and detail: John Donne's raffishly tilted hat; the thin-lipped smile of the wit John Harington; Ralegh beside his eight-year-old son, who will later die in search of gold in South America. They tell us also about the circumstances and status of the writer, and about the different sub-groups of the Elizabethan literary scene. They exude, as a collection, a certain historical atmosphere, a mood: perhaps an unexpected mood.

One thinks of the Elizabethan Age as a time of great national invigoration, a heady era of patriotism and poetry, of gaudiness and swagger, of expanding horizons both geographical and intellectual. This heroic view of the period is partly true, but is also propagandist – a propaganda put out by the Elizabethans themselves, gratefully swallowed by the Victorians, and still very much current. The writers seem to have expressed this surge of national confidence. In their work the very language quickens with new possibilities. They were in some measure the vehicles of this boom-time propaganda (this is especially true of the dramatists).

But there was another Elizabethan mood entirely, which they also expressed, which was compounded of scepticism, a sense of transience, and a generous dash of that other much-cultivated Elizabethan attribute, melancholy. It is this mix of zest and doubt which makes the period so fascinating. When the Globe theatre opened its doors in Southwark in 1599 it was to launch Shakespeare's jingoistic crowd-pleaser *Henry V*, but a couple of years later it was the moody, faltering, doubt-ridden Prince of

Denmark treading the boards, with his 'craven scruple of thinking too precisely' and his sense of 'something rotten' in the body politic.

Hamlet's mood of questioning, of nervy unrest, almost of vertigo in an age of such rapid transition, is also very Elizabethan. It is perhaps this darker flip-side which speaks to us today, which brings these authors so close to ourselves and our *fin-de-siècle* preoccupations. It is a mood one glimpses often in their portraits. There is not much sense of swashbuckling here. Cries of 'Gadzooks!' do not spring to mind. There is colour and finery, but the brilliance is somehow sombre, the swagger is tinged with melancholy. This is partly a matter of portrait conventions – a certain sternness was *de rigueur* – but the mood is nonetheless pervasive.

Chronologically this collection of portraits – and indeed this mood – can be described as 'late Elizabethan', though this shorthand needs some explanation. These writers are all Elizabethans, but most of them continued to work after the death of Elizabeth, in 1603, and are therefore Jacobean writers as well. (The youngest, Francis Beaumont, was born in 1584 and his writing career had scarcely begun before the Elizabethan age had ended.) Many of the portraits here are Jacobean in date; some are later copies. These chronological niceties should be noted, but often one is just thankful that these pictures have survived at all. So much from the period is lost. Writers of the stature of Thomas Kyd, John Lyly, Thomas Dekker, John Webster and Edmund Spenser are missing. No portrait of them survives; they are faceless. Others like Thomas Nashe and Robert Greene are known only from rough woodcuts printed in pamphlets. These are more like caricatures. They faithfully report certain physical features (Nashe's goofy teeth, Greene's long pointed beard shaped 'like a steeple') but these are grafted onto more generalised features.

There are obvious reasons for this paucity of visual record, chiefly the lowly status of writing as a profession. Indeed writing had only recently been regarded as a profession at all. Many of the writers included here were not portrayed *because* they were writers. They were either aristocrats, like the Earl of Oxford and the Countess of Pembroke; or courtly knights like Sidney, Ralegh, Harington and Overbury; or diplomats and politicians like Wotton and Bacon; or free-floating chancers and voyagers like the younger John Donne. Writing was for them an accomplishment, a pursuit, never a profession.

THOMAS NASHE
Unknown engraver, 1597

The dramatists we see here are the exceptions to this. Shakespeare, Marlowe, Jonson, Beaumont and Fletcher were all men of very middling origins, who largely depended on writing for their livelihood, and who attained a popular and cultural appeal far outstripping their social status. To these one adds Michael Drayton, who was a poet rather than a playwright. These are the professionals, the traders in words. Their costumes seem often to reflect this: simple, dark, functional. 'His habit was very

7

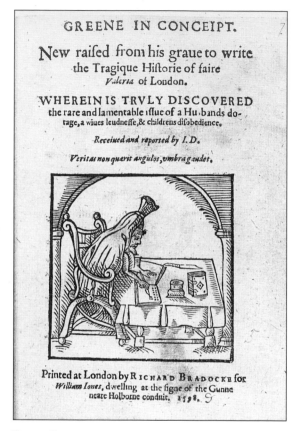

ROBERT GREENE
Unknown engraver, 1598

plain,' wrote the biographer John Aubrey of Ben Jonson. There are no
ruffs among them, but simple falling-band collars. This austerity of dress
hints at the persona of the scholar, a hint which makes subtle claims for a
superior status, an alternative to other connotations – the entertainer, the
verbal tumbler, the 'filthy playmaker' – which attended the profession.

These groups were to some extent discrete. The courtly writers all knew
one another; they mingled and jostled and plotted together. The profes-

sionals all knew one another too; they passed the time together in taverns and theatrical back-rooms, and among the booksellers' stalls of St Paul's Churchyard. There was some commerce between the two groups, but mostly in the context of patronage: Marlowe was part of the free-thinking clique (or 'school of atheism', as a contemporary called it) that met at Sir Walter Ralegh's house on the Strand; Drayton was a frequent guest of the Haringtons at Kelston House; Shakespeare put on a private performance of *As You Like It* for the Countess of Pembroke in 1603.

Another way of grouping these writers tells the following stark story: of the fifteen authors portrayed here, fourteen are men. It is also notable that at least seven of them spent time in prison, and four died violently (Sidney from war-wounds, Marlowe stabbed by a dagger, Overbury poisoned and Ralegh beheaded.) It was a tough time, and being a writer did not make it any easier.

In the brief biographical sketches that follow there is the usual mix of documentary and anecdotal evidence. Much of the latter comes from the great seventeenth-century memoirists – John Aubrey, Thomas Fuller, Sir Robert Naunton, Izaak Walton. These men were excellent historians, but also avid jotters-down of ephemera and gossip; their stories are irresistible but usually unverifiable. On the other hand, they were a lot closer to the Elizabethans than we are, and their sources were in some cases eye-witnesses. They are at least a rich repository of oral traditions.

This element of factual uncertainty is even more pronounced with the portraiture of the period. Actual documentary evidence is often slight, making conclusive identification of subjects difficult or impossible, as in the case of the portrait thought to be of Michael Drayton illustrated in this book. Our knowledge is always changing, too, as scholarship advances.

The most problematic work is perhaps the portrait belonging to Corpus Christi College, Cambridge, which is said to represent Christopher Marlowe. The young man in the portrait is unidentified in the inscription, which reads: *ANNO DŇI 1585 ÆTATIS SUAE 21/ QUOD ME NUTRIT ME DESTRUIT.*

The history of the painting between 1585, when it was painted, and 1953, when it was found poking out of a pile of builder's rubble in a court-yard in Cambridge, is a blank. It is thought that the sitter might be Marlowe because the dates fit with the inscription – he was twenty-one in

1585 – and because the portrait turned up at Corpus Christi College, where Marlowe was indeed a student in 1585. Add to this an intuitive sense of aptness: the sardonic gaze, the dandified gear, the haunting motto – *Quod me nutrit me destruit*: What feeds me destroys me – which seems to foreshadow his brief, lurid career. The evidence is tenuous but the notion is nonetheless compelling. It is hard now to detach this face from Marlowe: either it is him, or it is the mask he now wears when we see him in our imaginations.

The marvellous oil-painting called the 'Chandos portrait' is also unnamed, but though its identity as a portrait of Shakespeare remains unproven, it has a documentary pedigree that takes us almost back to the painting of it. It takes its name from the Chandos family, and was catalogued among their collection at Stowe in 1747. Its earlier provenance is summed up in an intriguing MS note by the eighteenth-century engraver and art-historian George Vertue:

> *The Picture of Shakespeare. Original of Mr Keyck of the Temple. He bought [it] for forty guineas of Mr Baterton, who bought of Sr W Davenant, to whom it was left by will of JohnTaylor … It was painted by Taylor, a player & painter contemp with Shakes & his intimate friend.*
>
> (Notebooks, I)

Assiduous detective work has fleshed out much of this history of ownership, from the barrister Robert Keck, who owned it in 1719, to the actor Thomas Betterton, and back to Sir William Davenant, the seventeenth-century poet and playwright who claimed to be Shakespeare's godson and/or illegitimate child. The identity of the artist himself remains elusive. Attention has focused on a John Taylor who was a young actor with the Paul's Boys in 1598; and a John Taylor who was a member of the Company of Painter-Stainers by 1626, and who died in 1651. Might these perhaps be the same John Taylor, and might he be the artist described by Vertue as both 'player & painter'?

It is possible. One cannot be certain, as so often with the Elizabethans. We look on his picture; his picture looks back; the eyes that fix us do not suggest much faith in certainties.

Select Bibliography

L. Cust, 'The Portraits of Sir Walter Raleigh', *Walpole Society*, VIII, 1920, pp. 6–7.

Mary Edmond, 'The Chandos Portrait: A Suggested Painter', *Burlington Magazine*, vol. CXXIX, 1982, pp. 146–9.

David Evett, *Literature and the Visual Arts in Tudor England*, Athens, Georgia and London, 1990.

Lucy Gent, *Picture and Poetry 1560–1620: Relations Between Literature and the Visual Arts in the English Renaissance*, Leamington Spa, 1981.

R.W. Goulding, 'Wriothesley Portraits', *Walpole Society*, VIII, 1920, pp. 51–62.

Karen Hearn (ed.), *Dynasties: Painting in Tudor and Jacobean England 1530–1630*, exh. cat., Tate Gallery, London, 1995.

A.M. Hind, *Engraving in England in the 16th and 17th Centuries*; Part I: *The Tudor Period*; Part II: *The Reign of James I*, Cambridge, 1952, 1955.

Maurice Howard, *The Tudor Image*, London, 1995.

Darren Emerson Lay, 'The Taylor of St Paul's: Who Painted the Chandos Portrait?', *Times Literary Supplement*, 24 May 1994, p.17.

David Piper, *Seventeenth-Century Portraits in the National Portrait Gallery*, London, 1963.

David Piper, *O Sweet Mr Shakespeare I'll Have His Picture: The Changing Image of Shakespeare's Person, 1600–1800*, National Portrait Gallery, 1964.

David Piper, *The English Face*, London, 1992.

Roy Strong, *The English Icon: Elizabethan and Jacobean Portraiture*, 1969.

Roy Strong, *Tudor and Jacobean Portraits*, London, 1969.

Roy Strong, with contributions from V. J. Murrell, *Artists of the Tudor Court: The Portrait Miniature Rediscovered, 1520–1620*, Victoria and Albert Museum, 1983.

Roy Strong, *The English Renaissance Miniature*, 1983.

Roy Strong, 'The Leicester House Miniatures: Robert Sidney, 1st Earl of Leicester and his Circle', *Burlington Magazine*, vol. CXXVII, 1985, pp. 694–701.

Roy Strong, 'Sidney's Appearance Reconsidered', *Sir Philip Sidney's Achievements*, ed. Allen, Baker-Smith and Kinney, New York, 1990.

WILLIAM SHAKESPEARE
Attributed to John Taylor, early 17th century

WILLIAM SHAKESPEARE (1564–1616)

Universally considered the greatest of Elizabethan writers – 'the soul of the age' as Ben Jonson put it – Shakespeare remains a somewhat shadowy figure. He did not attract personal publicity in the way that Marlowe and Jonson did, nor did he pursue courtly preferment. The acquisition of a family coat-of-arms (motto 'Non Sans Droit', parodied by Jonson as 'Not Without Mustard') and the steady accumulation of property are the documented signs of his success.

'He was not a company-keeper ... [and] would not be debosh'd [debauched],' says John Aubrey. He devoted his life to the theatre, as actor and company-shareholder as well as writer. His collected works, *Mr William Shakespeare's Comedies, Histories, and Tragedies*, better known as the 'First Folio' of 1623, contains thirty-six plays. A later edition (1664) added *Pericles* to the canon, and there are other, earlier works which may yet prove to be his.

Born in Stratford, the son of a glover, Shakespeare was brought up in a discreetly Catholic family. He married a local woman, Anne Hathwey or Hathaway, by whom he had three children. His whereabouts during the 1580s are unknown – there is no documentary record of him between 1582 (his marriage) and 1587 (a property document). It is thought he was in Lancashire, serving in Catholic households, and that he is the William 'Shakeshafte' who is mentioned in Sir Alexander Houghton's will of 1581 and who probably served as one of Sir Thomas Hesketh's players at Rufford Hall thereafter. However, Aubrey says 'he had been in his younger years a schoolmaster in the country.' He is certainly the 'Shake-scene' attacked by the writer Robert Greene in 1592, by which time he had achieved prominence, in London, as an actor and author. Greene writes:

> There is an upstart crow beautified with our feathers, that with his 'Tiger's heart wrapped in a player's hide' supposes he is as well able to bombast out a blank verse as the best of you; and being an absolute Johannes Factotum, [jack of all trades] is in his own conceit that only Shake-scene in a country.

(A Groatsworth of Wit, 1592)

A few months later, the author Henry Chettle, who edited Greene's *Groatsworth* after the latter's death, made some amends for this, saying:

Myself have seen his demeanour no less civil than he excellent in the quality he professes. Besides, divers of worship have reported his uprightness of dealing, which argues his honesty, and his facetious grace in writing, which approves his art.

(Kind-Heart's Dream, 1592)

Shakespeare's first published works were poems rather than plays – *Venus and Adonis* (1593) and *The Rape of Lucrece* (1594), both dedicated to his patron, Henry Wriothesley, 3rd Earl of Southampton. From 1594 he was an actor and shareholder in the Lord Chamberlain's Men, which became the King's Men in 1603. His plays were performed at the Theatre and Curtain in Shoreditch; at the Globe in Southwark; and latterly at the private theatre of Blackfriars, for which more intimate setting his last plays were written. *The Tempest* (c.1611) has the air of a farewell ('Our revels now are ended …'), but Shakespeare later collaborated with John Fletcher on *Henry VIII* (c.1613), and may have also contributed to another of Fletcher's plays, *Two Noble Kinsmen* (c.1614).

John Aubrey describes him as 'a handsome, well-shaped man, very good company, and of a very ready and pleasant smooth wit.' Probably the best-known image of him is the engraving by Martin Droeshout illustrated in the Introduction. This was first published in the 1623 Folio but may have been based on a lost miniature: the stiff wired collar suggests a date of 1610–16 for the original. Much more atmospheric is the 'Chandos Portrait', attributed to John Taylor, illustrated here and discussed in the Introduction. The features are similar to those of the Droeshout, but the painting is full of drama – the dark, almost Latin cast; the piratical earring, the wary gaze.

According to tradition, Shakespeare died at New Place, Stratford, after over-indulging in the company of Jonson and Michael Drayton: 'Drayton and Ben Jonson had a merry meeting, and, it seems, drank too hard, for Shakespeare died of a fever there contracted.' (Revd John Ward, Vicar of Stratford, c.1662) The bust of Shakespeare incorporated into his monument in Holy Trinity church in Stratford was *in situ* by 1623 (it is referred to by Leonard Digges in prefatory verses in the First Folio). It is said to have been sculpted by Gerard Johnson the Younger, and may be based on a death-mask. It is the least attractive of the images of Shakespeare: plump and bourgeois.

WILLIAM SHAKESPEARE
Plaster copy after Gerard Johnson's marble effigy at Stratford-upon-Avon, c.1620

CHRISTOPHER MARLOWE (1564–93)

❧

Kit Marlowe was the wild boy of Elizabethan literature, the wayward young genius cut short in his prime. He was just twenty-nine years old when he was stabbed to death in a dockside lodging-house at Deptford in south-east London.

During his brief life, Marlowe was both revered and reviled: 'Wit sent from heaven but vices sent from hell.' His 'wit' survives in half a dozen plays, including that great Elizabethan spine-chiller *Dr Faustus*, and some fine lyric poetry. His 'vices' were (or were said to be) atheism, blasphemy and homosexuality. All of them were considered vices – indeed crimes – at this time: dangerous positions to take, dangerous tastes to have.

Born in Canterbury, the son of a shoemaker, he was an exact contemporary of Shakespeare. They later knew one another: during his lifetime Marlowe was the more famous. He studied at King's School, Canterbury, and won a scholarship to Corpus Christi College, Cambridge. His university career was chequered. In 1587 the authorities accused him of subversive Catholic activities, and refused to grant his MA degree. Their decision was overturned by the Privy Council, who furnished an exonerating letter saying Marlowe 'had done her Majesty good service' in certain confidential 'affairs'. This suggests that Marlowe had already been recruited into the government's extensive network of anti-Catholic spies.

Despite Marlowe's considerable fame in his lifetime, no documented portraits of him are known. If the Corpus Christi portrait of 1585 (discussed in the Introduction) does indeed represent Marlowe, it may relate to this first spell of government service. In his fine dress, the young man in the portrait does not look like a shilling-a-week Cambridge scholar, but he may look like an ambitious young meddler in the dangerous waters of Elizabethan politics. Marlowe's college buttery accounts for 1585 are extant, and show an unexpected flush of spending money.

Marlowe's earliest theatrical success was *Tamburlaine the Great*, performed in 1587. He hastily cobbled up a sequel; at a performance of the latter, by the Admiral's Men, an accidentally loaded gun went off onstage, killing two of the spectators. Only five other plays are known: *Dido, Queen*

?CHRISTOPHER MARLOWE
Unknown artist, 1585

NVTRIT
RVIT

SIR FRANCIS WALSINGHAM
Attributed to John de Critz, the Elder, *c.*1587

of Carthage, Dr Faustus, The Jew of Malta, Massacre at Paris, and *Edward II.*
This is the probable order of their composition, but no dates are known.
His plays are full of passionate poetry – 'his high-astounding terms', as he
put it – and full of spectacle and violence, but their undertone of irony and
black humour, and their rapidity of action, make them very modern. T.S.
Eliot described his style as not so much tragedy as a kind of 'serious, even
savage farce'.

In 1589 Marlowe was imprisoned after a sword-fight in which an innkeeper's son, William Bradley, was killed (though not by him). In 1591 he was sharing a chamber in London with the playwright Thomas Kyd. In 1592, he was arrested in the Netherlands on a charge of 'coining' (counterfeiting money) and was deported under escort to be examined by Lord Burghley. He was also accused of 'intent to go to the enemy', in other words of defecting to the Spanish Catholic forces. On this occasion, as at Cambridge, he escaped punishment: this is probably another episode in Marlowe's shadowy career as a spy. In the same year he was in trouble for disturbing the peace in Shoreditch, and, on a visit to Canterbury in September, for menacing a tailor named Corkine with 'a dagger and a staff'.

Among his many friends were the poets Thomas Watson and George Chapman, the pamphleteer Thomas Nashe, and the scientists Thomas Harriot and Walter Warner, and among his patrons were intellectual noblemen like Lord Strange and the Earl of Northumberland, the adventurer Sir Walter Ralegh, and Thomas Walsingham, a young cousin of the spy-master Sir Francis Walsingham.

His connection with the freethinking clique of Ralegh and Northumberland brought him into political danger. It was said he 'had read the atheist lecture' to them, and had circulated a 'book against the Trinity'. In May 1593 a series of charges were laid against him by the spy Richard Baines, who had been the cause of his arrest in the Netherlands. The 'Baines Note' is a terrific itemisation of Marlowe's 'damnable opinions' and heresies, among them:

… That Moses was but a juggler
… That the first beginning of religion was only to keep men in awe
… That Christ was a bastard and his mother dishonest
… That St John the Evangelist was bedfellow to Christ, and leaned always in his bosom, and that he used him as the sinners of Sodoma
… That all they that love not tobacco & boys were fools

On 12 May 1593 his former chamber-fellow Thomas Kyd was arrested and tortured. He too spoke out against Marlowe:

It was his custom … to jest at the divine scriptures, jibe at prayers, and strive in argument to frustrate and confute what hath been spoke and writ by prophets.

Some of Kyd's comments on Marlowe suggest a genuine recoiling. 'He was intemperate & of a cruel heart', Kyd said, and much given to 'attempting sudden privy injuries on men'. On 20 May Marlowe was himself summoned before the Privy Council, but remained at liberty, on bail.

Ten days later, he met up with three men at a lodging-house in Deptford. They were shady characters: spies and fraudsters, his colleagues in the underworld. They dined together in a private room, they walked in the garden. At about seven o'clock in the evening Marlowe was fatally stabbed through the right eye by one of his companions, Ingram Frizer. According to the coroner's inquest, they had quarrelled over the 'reckoning', or bill, for the day's food and drink. Frizer was acquitted on a plea of self-defence, but questions remain about the true cause and motive of the killing.

Marlowe's fellow poets mourned the loss of the 'Muses' darling' (George Peele), of 'neat Marlowe' – neat in the sense of unadulterated, like neat whisky – 'whose raptures were all air and fire' (Michael Drayton). But to the Puritans, who loathed him and all he stood for, his violent and sordid end was a 'manifest sign of God's judgement' upon him. 'See what a hook the Lord put in the nostrils of this barking dog', thundered the preacher Thomas Beard with ghoulish satisfaction. (This Dr Beard was many years later Oliver Cromwell's schoolteacher.)

Shakespeare quoted from Marlowe's work in *As You Like It* (c.1599); in the same play he addressed him as the 'dead shepherd', and the riddling lines of the clown Touchstone may be a comment on the circumstances of Marlowe's death: 'It strikes a man more dead than a great reckoning in a little room'.

BEN JONSON (?1572–1637)

Ben Jonson was the great comic genius of the age. His career as dramatist, masque-writer and poet spans four decades and three reigns, and produced nearly forty plays. He was a big-gestured, quarrelsome, heavy-drinking man:

> *He would many times exceed in drink (Canary was his beloved liquor) then he would tumble home to bed, and when he had thoroughly perspired, then to study. I have seen his studying-chair, which was of straw, such as old women used.*
>
> (John Aubrey, Lives)

Yet his writing is more punctiliously 'classical' than that of any of his contemporaries. John Dryden singled him out as 'the greatest man of the last age', but found in him something difficult and off-putting, adding: 'I admire him, but I love Shakespeare'.

BEN JONSON, by, or after Abraham van Blyenberch, *c.*1617

According to his own account, Jonson was the son of a Protestant minister, from a Scottish family which had forfeited its estates during the reign of Mary Tudor. He was 'posthumous born' a month after the death of his father. His mother married a bricklayer, Robert Brett; he was 'brought up poorly', on Harts Horn Lane in Westminster. An unknown benefactor enabled him to study at Westminster School, under the great scholar William Camden. In his youth he was variously an apprentice bricklayer, a soldier in the Low Countries, and a strolling actor. In 1597 he was imprisoned for his part in writing a 'lewd' and 'seditious' play, *The Isle of Dogs*, part-written by Thomas Nashe; and again the following year, after killing the actor Gabriel Spenser in a sword-fight.

With *Every Man in his Humour* (1598), performed by the Lord Chamberlain's Men with Shakespeare in the cast, Jonson began the long run of successful, brilliantly crafted, topical comedies, including *Volpone* (1605), *The Alchemist* (1610) and *Bartholomew Fair* (1614). Around the turn of the century he was involved in the public mud-slinging of the 'War of the Theatres' and traded insults with rival playwrights Thomas Dekker and John Marston. Dekker described Jonson's face as 'like a rotten russet apple when 'tis bruised', and a voice which 'sounds so i'th'nose'. At gentlemen's tables he would 'fling epigrams, emblems and play-speeches about him like hail-stones' (*Satiromastix*, 1601).

In 1605 Jonson was in prison again, as a result of slighting references to King James and his 'Scottish Knights' in his London comedy *Eastward Ho!*, and later that year was peripherally involved in the government's investigation of the Gunpowder Plot. He espoused Catholicism for some years, then in about 1610 returned to the Protestant fold: 'At his first communion, in token of true reconciliation, he drank out all the full cup of wine' (William Drummond). In 1619 he walked from London to Scotland (he bought a new pair of shoes in Darlington), and stayed at Hawthornden with the poet William Drummond, who left this sketch of him:

> *He is a great lover and praiser of himself, a contemner and scorner of others, given rather to lose a friend than a jest, jealous of every word and action of those about him (especially after drink, which is one of the elements in which he liveth), a dissembler of ill parts which reign in him, a bragger of some good that he wanteth, thinketh nothing well but what either he himself or some of*

BEN JONSON
Robert Vaughan, after 1632

his friends and countrymen hath said or done. He is passionately kind and angry, careless either to gain or keep, vindictive, but if he be well answered, at himself.

A portrait of Jonson by the Dutch artist Abraham van Blyenberch is mentioned in an inventory of the Duke of Buckingham's pictures in 1635, two years before Jonson's death; this may be the portrait in the National Portrait Gallery illustrated here, and there are also various later copies. Blyenberch was working in England between 1617 and 1620, so in this image we probably see Jonson in his late forties. The engraving by Robert Vaughan is from around the same time. It seems to bear out John Aubrey's comment that 'Ben Jonson had one eye lower than t'other, and bigger', but it may, equally, be the source of Aubrey's description.

Bed-ridden from a stroke, Jonson lived his last years at the Gate House at Westminster, with a drunken housekeeper and a pet fox. His epitaph in Poet's Corner reads simply 'O Rare Ben Jonson'.

Judicis argutum qui non formidat

acumen

FRANCIS
BEAVMONT Efq

Æ Ætat Circ XXV AD 1615

Geo. Vertue Sculp 1729

Celsissimo Principi LEONELLO DUCI de DORSET &c.
Nobilissimo Ordinis Periscelides Equiti
Hanc Tabulam ad Archetypum in ipsius Ædibus expressam   Humil. D.D.D. G. Vertue

FRANCIS BEAUMONT (1584–1616) AND
JOHN FLETCHER (1579–1625)

❦

Beaumont and Fletcher wrote a dozen plays together in the early years of the seventeenth century, among them *The Knight of the Burning Pestle* (c.1607), *Philaster* (1609) and *The Maid's Tragedy* (1610–11). Though both wrote solo-works, they are best known as collaborators:

> *John Fletcher and Francis Beaumont esquire, like Castor and Pollux (most happy when in conjunction), raised the English to equal the Athenian and Roman theatre; Beaumont bringing the ballast of judgement, Fletcher the sail of fantasy, both compounding a poet to admiration.*
>
> (Thomas Fuller, Worthies of England, 1660)

Beaumont was the younger son of a well-to-do Leicestershire magistrate. He left Oxford without taking a degree and in 1600 came to London, where he enrolled at the fashionable Inner Temple. He was part of Ben Jonson's circle, and was one of the famous company of wits who met at the Mermaid tavern in Bread Street. His earliest play, *The Woman Hater* (c.1605) is a Jonsonian 'comedy of humours'. His friendship with Fletcher dates from around this time:

> *They lived together on the Bankside, not far from the playhouse [i.e. the Globe], both batchelors; lay together; had one wench in the house between them, which they did so admire; the same clothes and cloak etc. between them.*
>
> (John Aubrey, Lives)

Beaumont married advantageously and retired from London to Kent in about 1612. The countryside did not suit him. He wrote to Jonson: 'the little wit I had is lost'. The days of wine and repartee at the Mermaid seemed suddenly distant:

> *… What things have we seen,*
> *Done at the Mermaid? Heard words that have been*
> *So nimble and so full of subtle flame*
> *As if that everyone from whom they came*
> *Had meant to put his whole wit in a jest,*
> *And had resolved to live a fool the rest*
> *Of his dull life …*
>
> (Verse-letter to Ben Jonson, c.1612)

There is a portrait of Beaumont at Knole, Kent, which dates from 1615, showing a strong, handsome face, expressive hands, and the twirled mous-tachios and square-cut beard which are his trademark features in later engravings, such as the early eighteenth-century one by George Vertue illustrated here. Beaumont died at the age of thirty-two. Jonson sourly remarked to William Drummond: 'Beaumont loved too much himself and his own verses.'

John Fletcher was from a family of preachers and writers. His father Richard Fletcher was chaplain at the execution of Mary Stuart in 1587, and later became Bishop of London; his uncle Giles Fletcher was a scholar and diplomat, and wrote a celebrated book about Russia (*Of the Russe Commonwealth*, 1591); his cousins Phineas and Giles junior were both poets. Fletcher himself studied at Corpus Christi College, Cambridge (Marlowe's former college), but his studies were curtailed when his father died in debt in 1596. His huge output of plays – in all he wrote or co-wrote over fifty – was doubtless dictated by financial need.

From two former actors, John Lowin and Joseph Taylor, we get a glimpse of Fletcher mingling with the audience at one of his plays: 'we have know him unconcerned, and to have wished it had been none of his', but if the play went down well 'he, as well as the thronged theatre (in despite of his innate modesty), applauding this rare issue of his brain'.

A story is told by Bishop Fuller:

> *Meeting once in a tavern to contrive the rude draft of a tragedy, Fletcher undertook to kill the king herein, whose words being overheard by a listener (though his loyalty not to be blamed herein) he was accused of high treason, till the mistake soon appearing, that the plot was only against a dramatic and scenical king, all wound off in merriment.*

This is doubtless apocryphal, but suggests the parlousness of play-writing in a time of censorship and surveillance.

The portrait of Fletcher in the collection of the Earl of Clarendon (of which the National Portrait Gallery portrait illustrated here is a later copy) shows him in costume of *c*.1620; he was then in his early forties. He has light brown wavy hair and a wispy beard. He died in Southwark, and was buried at St Saviour's, now Southwark Cathedral:

JOHN FLETCHER, Unknown artist, late 17th or early 18th century

Invited to go with a knight into Norfolk or Suffolk in the plague time,1625,
[he] stayed but to make himself a suit of clothes, and while it was making,
fell sick of the plague and died.

(John Aubrey, Lives)

According to tradition Fletcher's friend the playwright Philip Massinger
was buried 'in the same grave' when he died in 1640.

SIR PHILIP SIDNEY
Unknown artist, c.1576?

SIR PHILIP SIDNEY (1554–86) AND
MARY HERBERT, COUNTESS OF PEMBROKE (1561–1621)

A ttractive, talented and well-connected, Philip and Mary Sidney were figureheads (Philip as poet, Mary as patron) of a certain kind of Elizabethan writing: refined, philosophical, pastoral, a world away from the rougher commercial milieu of the playwrights and pamphleteers.

The nephew of the Earl of Leicester and (from 1583) the son-in-law of Sir Francis Walsingham, Sir Philip Sidney was 'the most accomplished cavalier of his time'. He was regarded as the Elizabethan ideal of the soldier-poet, the man of action and refinement: 'Mars and Mercury fell at variance whose servant he should be'.

> With the state of his person framed by a natural propension to arms, he was so highly prized in the esteem of the Queen that she thought the court deficient without him ... He was a noble and matchless gentleman, and it may be justly said of him that he seemed to be born only to that which he went about: Versatilis ingenii, as Plutarch hath it.
>
> (Sir Robert Naunton, Fragmenta Regalia,1633)

Sidney's sonnet-sequence, *Astrophel and Stella*, describes his illicit passion for Penelope Rich, and offers advice pertinent to all writers: '"Fool," said my Muse to me, "Look in thy heart and write."' His prose-work, *Arcadia*, was influential in creating a fashion for the pastoral. He also wrote a fine *Defence of Poetry* in answer to Puritan anti-literary diatribes. Fighting the Spanish in the Netherlands, Sidney was wounded in action at Zutphen – reputedly giving his water-bottle to another soldier, saying 'Thy necessity is yet greater than mine' – and died a month later at Arnheim, aged thirty-two. His funeral in London was one of the great displays of Elizabethan pageantry.

The poet Matthew Roydon, who knew Sidney, spoke of his 'sweet attractive kind of grace ' (*A Friend's Passion*, c.1586), but Ben Jonson, who is unlikely to have known him, said 'Sir P Sidney was no pleasant man in countenance, his face being spoiled by pimples, and of high blood, and long.' (*Conversations with Drummond*, 1619)

Despite his short life, a number of portraits of Sidney survive. The illustrated portrait, which may be an early posthumous copy of one at Longleat House, Wiltshire, shows him at the age of twenty-two in martial guise, with a decorated steel gorget, or armoured neckpiece, below his ruff. The hair colour just about corresponds with Aubrey's description of it as 'a dark amber colour'. The portrait originally belonged to Sir William Russell, Sidney's friend, who was with the poet when he was wounded at Zutphen.

Sidney's younger sister Mary was married at the age of sixteen to Henry Herbert, 2nd Earl of Pembroke, who was nearly thirty years older than she. She was his third wife. 'Fair and witty', she became 'the greatest patroness of wit and learning of any lady in her time'. (John Aubrey, *Lives*) Her country seat, Wilton House, 'was like a College'. Among her protégés were the poets Samuel Daniel and Nicholas Breton, but the Grub-streeter Tom Nashe, who had edited an unauthorised edition of *Astrophel and Stella*, was sent packing. She jealously guarded the memory and literary effects of her brother. She oversaw the definitive edition of the *Arcadia* (1593), much of which had been written in her company at Wilton.

Mary's elder son William Herbert, later 3rd Earl, was also a patron of poets, but was not the 'Mr W.H.' described as the 'only begetter' of Shakespeare's *Sonnets*. Her younger son Philip was named after her brother: it was scurrilously said he was Sidney's son, though 'he inherited not the wit of either brother or sister'.

MARY HERBERT, COUNTESS OF PEMBROKE
Nicholas Hilliard, *c.*1590

MARY HERBERT, COUNTESS OF PEMBROKE
Simon van der Passe, 1618

The miniature by Nicholas Hilliard shows her in about 1590, at the age of twenty-nine, and wearing a large white ruff. The portrait is a couple of inches wide, and is backed with a snippet of playing-card (Two of Spades). It is the only known likeness of her prior to the formidable old lady portrayed by Simon van der Passe in 1618, three years before her death. 'She had a pretty, sharp, oval face,' says Aubrey, and hair 'of a reddish yellow'.

JOHN DONNE (1572–1631)

۰۰۰

If the chivalrous soldier-poet Philip Sidney was the Elizabethans' idea of the perfect all-rounder, John Donne is perhaps a more modern version, with his mix of intellectual rigour and sexual passion, and his evolution from the cynical philanderer of the *Songs and Sonnets* to the great meditator on sin and redemption in the sermons he preached at St Paul's Cathedral.

Donne was born into a fervently Catholic family: his mother was a relative of Sir Thomas More and a sister of the Jesuit leader Jasper Heywood. The family lived on Bread Street, London, close to the Mermaid tavern. Donne's father, an ironmonger, died when he was four. His mother married a Catholic physician, Dr John Syminges. As a 'recusant' (literally a refuser, i.e. a Catholic), Donne was able to study at university but not to take a degree. He went up to Hart Hall, Oxford, in 1582, and probably studied at Cambridge as well. At the age of twenty he was admitted to Lincoln's Inn, nominally to study law but also to cultivate himself as a poet, wit and man about town, since the Inns of Court were a kind of 'finishing school' for young men.

The superb, raffish portrait of Donne as melancholy lover dates from the mid-1590s. (In his will he left this portrait to Robert, Earl of Ancrum, describing it as 'that picture of mine taken in the shadows'; it descended directly to its present owner, the Marquis of Lothian, but was not identified as Donne until 1959; it had been mislabelled 'Duns Scotus'!)

Donne's physical appearance is described by Izaak Walton:

Of stature moderately tall, of a straight and equally proportioned body, to which all his words and actions gave an inexpressible addition of comeliness.

(Life of Donne, 1681)

Donne's earliest surviving poems, the *Satires*, also date from the time of the Lothian portrait, and are very acerbic and topical but written in his characteristic knotty style. The darkness of their mood is thought to relate to a period of spiritual and psychological angst when Donne renounced his deep-dyed Catholicism. His younger brother Henry had been arrested in 1593 for harbouring Catholic priests, and died in prison.

In 1596 Donne was among the gentleman adventurers who sailed with Essex's squadron in the famous assault on Cadiz. The following year he

JOHN DONNE, unknown artist, *c*.1595

was at sea again in the Azores expedition under Ralegh. On this voyage he sent his verse-letters, 'The Calm' and 'The Storm', to his Inns of Court friend Christopher Brooke. His career prospered: he became secretary to Sir Thomas Egerton, Lord Keeper of the Great Seal, and entered Parliament in 1601 as MP for Brackley.

At the end of that year he secretly married Lady Egerton's seventeen-year-old niece, Ann More, and was summarily dismissed from service. He commemorated his fall in the famous doggerel, 'John Donne/Ann Donne/ Undonne'. For some years the couple lived a threadbare life in a cottage in Mitcham, Surrey, producing children at an alarming rate (Ann died

JOHN DONNE, unknown artist after Isaac
Oliver's miniature of 1616

giving birth to their twelfth child in 1617). He was supported by various
patrons, notably the Drurys of Hawstead, Suffolk, and Sir Henry Chute,
but remained in a kind of social wilderness. His verse darkened and grew
more religious: the *Holy Sonnets* (*c*.1610–11) and *Anniversaries* (1612–13).

In 1615 Donne took holy orders, and King James, who had considered
him untrustworthy in political matters, made him chaplain-in-ordinary to
the royal household. He became Dr Donne by virtue of a Doctorate of
Divinity awarded him by Cambridge University, though this was at the
King's insistence; indeed, an overtone of careerism hangs over Donne's
entry into the church.

The National Portrait Gallery's portrait, a copy of a miniature by Isaac
Oliver dated 1616 (Royal Collection) shows Donne at this time: a sharp-
bearded, punctilious-looking man in his forties. The expression seems to
be edged with disappointments.

In 1621, through the offices of the King's favourite, the Duke of Buckingham, Donne was made Dean of St Paul's. He was the greatest preacher
of his day. His most famous sermon begins 'No man is an island ...'.

MICHAEL DRAYTON (1563–1631)

A Warwickshire man, Michael Drayton described himself as 'nobly bred' and 'well allied'. This referred not to his family, of which nothing is known, but to his boyhood in the household of Sir Henry Goodere of Powlesworth, where he was a page-boy. According to John Aubrey, his father was a butcher (but Aubrey said the same about Shakespeare's father, who was actually a glover.)

'Golden-mouthed Drayton' was widely admired, both as a poet and as a man of integrity:

> Among scholars, soldiers, poets and all sorts of people [he] is held for a man of virtuous disposition, honest conversation, and well-governed carriage.
>
> (Francis Meres, Palladis Tamia,1598)

Drayton was a plain-speaking, somewhat reclusive man. Of publishers he wrote: 'They are a company of base knaves whom I both scorn and kick at'. He wrote passionate love poems – including the famous sonnet, 'Since there's no help, come let us kiss and part' – but remained a bachelor. A single unhappy passion seems to have dominated his personal life. The object of his affections (possibly his patron's daughter, Anne Goodere) is hymned for over thirty years, from the sonnets of *Idea* (1593) to the verse-epistle 'Of His Lady's Not Coming To Town' (1627). He was small in stature, with what he describes as a 'swart and melancholy face'.

Drayton's most famous poem was 'Poly-Olbion' (1st part 1613, 2nd part 1622), an immense 'chorographicall [i.e. topographical] description' of British 'tracts, rivers, mountains, forests' and other features. He was already 'penning' the poem in 1598, according to Meres, so it took him at least twenty-four years to complete.

Among Drayton's friends were Francis Beaumont, William Drummond, and the poet and physician Thomas Lodge, and he was often a guest of Sir John Harington. He was also a personal friend of Shakespeare, and it is said they dined together shortly before Shakespeare's death.

Drayton's relations with Ben Jonson were difficult. He shared something of Jonson's truculence; Jonson told Drummond that 'Drayton feared him, and he esteemed not of him', but later sublimated these tensions into a fine poem, 'The Vision of Ben Jonson, on the Muses of His Friend M. Drayton' (1627):

Æ: SVÆ. 30.   A.D. 1599.

CALLED MICHAEL DRAYTON
Unknown artist, ?1599

It hath been questioned, Michael, if I be
A friend at all; or, if at all, to thee;
Because who make the question have not seen
Those ambling visits pass in verse between
Thy muse and mine, as they expect. 'Tis true:
You have not writ to me, nor I to you;
And though I now begin, 'tis not to rub
Haunch against haunch, or rise a rhyming club
About the town. This reckoning I will pay ...

Drayton died in poverty, but was buried with honours at Westminster Abbey. The National Portrait Gallery's painting illustrated here shows a mild, pale, sensitive-looking man, with auburn hair and the poet's symbolic garland of bay leaves.

The identification as Drayton is uncertain: it was first suggested that it represented him by Lady Mary Thompson, its owner in the nineteenth century. When x-rayed in 1963, another portrait entirely was revealed beneath: a saturnine face, quite unlike other pictures of Drayton (though curiously matching his own description of himself as 'swart [i.e. dark] and melancholy'.) The inscriptions are later additions, so that the date of 1599 is also uncertain, though it seems right for the costume. The portrait has a strong facial resemblance to the older, sterner-looking Drayton of William Hole's engraving, done in 1613 and first published in the 1619 edition of Drayton's poems.

SIR JOHN HARINGTON (1561–1612)

The poet and wit Sir John Harington was the Queen's godson. His father, John, was a confidant of Henry VIII, married one of the king's illegitimate daughters, Etheldreda Malte, and cultivated a close relationship with Princess Elizabeth which was rewarded when she came to the throne. The younger Harington studied at Eton and King's College, Cambridge, and later at Lincoln's Inn. He was popular at court, a noted epigrammist and a *risqué* conversationalist – a kind of intellectual jester.

Harrington's fine translation of the Italian love-epic *Orlando Furioso* was published in 1591. According to tradition, he first translated some erotic passages, and circulated them at court; the Queen made him translate the rest as a penance. His much-loved dog, Bungey, features on the decorated title-page.

In 1596 Harington published a curious book – part-burlesque, part-technical manual – about lavatories, *The Metamorphosis of Ajax*. (Ajax puns on 'a jakes', or privy.) Banished once more from court as a result of this publication, he retired to his Somerset home, Kelston House, near Bath. He threw in his lot with the Earl of Essex, went with him to Ireland in 1598, and was knighted by him. Harington steered a skilful course between the Queen and the rebellious Earl, and so (as he put it) escaped 'shipwreck on the Essex coast'.

The Queen called him 'that saucy poet, my godson' and forgave him effronteries that others would not have dared to attempt. His cousin Robert Markham warned him: 'That damnable uncovered honesty of yours will mar your fortune'. His miscellaneous writings, *Nugae Antiquae*, were collected by a descendant, Revd Henry Harington, and published between 1769 and 1774.

The portrait opposite, attributed to Hieronimo Custodis, catches the mordant courtly joker, with his thin laconic mouth and his sharp-pointed *pic à devant* beard.

SIR JOHN HARINGTON
Attributed to Hieronimo Custodis, *c.*1590–5

THE
Portraicture
of Sir
THOMAS
OVERBVRY
Knight.
ÆTAT. 32.

Renold Elstrack Sculpsit.

Are to Be sould by Iohn Hind
at the black Bull in Cornhill neere the Royall
Exchange.

Those Swan-like notes, sung so insurely
to thy vntimely fall, proue most exact
Lines drawne from life: & thy swift Tragedie
showes but time owne Soules Prophecie in Act.
Thy Name, and Vertues liue: To kill thy Mould
was all, Imprisonment, and Poyson could.

But thy more-heauenly-Self, from double Baines
sett free (at once) Thy Body, and thy Tower
In that Supreme vnpartiall Court remaines,
ouer nor Ambition, Enuy, Lust haue power:
Redeem'd from poysonous plotts from Witches Charmes
from Westons & thy Apothecaries harmes. W.B.

SIR THOMAS OVERBURY (1581–1613)

❦

Overbury is remembered less for his literary attainments, which were slight, than for the lurid and still somewhat mysterious circumstances of his death, by poison, in the Tower of London, at the age of thirty-two. He had risen on the coat-tails of King James's favourite, Robert Carr. They met in Edinburgh in 1601 when Carr was a mere page-boy, and he was Carr's confidant during the latter's dizzying rise to courtly eminence as the Earl of Somerset. Queen Anne described him jokingly as Carr's 'governor'. A contemporary noted that Carr could not 'pursue any measure without the advice and concurrence of his friend, nor could Overbury enjoy any felicity but in the company of him he loved'.

In 1607 Overbury received a lucrative gift of some salt-works in Droitwich formerly owned by the attainted Gunpowder Plotter, Robert Winter; in 1608 he was made 'Sewer' in the King's household; and on 19 June 1608 he was knighted.

Quod me nutrit me destruit (What feeds me destroys me) was a favourite Elizabethan motto (and was inscribed on the portrait which may represent Marlowe); so it proved for Overbury. His protector Carr turned against him and destroyed him. The cause of the breach was Overbury's opposition to Carr's controversial marriage. Carr had fallen for the voluptuous Frances Howard, who had shocked polite society by divorcing the 3rd Earl of Essex on the grounds of his impotence. (She had undergone a virginity test, though the general opinion on that was summed up by the Prince of Wales, who refused to pick up her glove from the dance-floor, saying 'it had been stretched' by too many others.)

The couple engineered Overbury's imprisonment in the Tower, where he was slowly poisoned by doctors and apothecaries in their pay. According to the apothecary Franklin, white arsenic was the chief poison used, but 'aquafortis, mercury, powder of diamonds, lapis costitus, great spiders and cantherides' were also among the ingredients with which his food was spiked. The *coup de grâce* was 'a clyster [enema] of corrosive sublimate' administered to him on 14 September 1613; he died early the following morning.

A contemporary wrote, a few weeks after Overbury's death, in terms which suggest the bleakness of political disgrace:

SIR THOMAS OVERBURY, Renold Elstrack, *c.*1615

FRANCES HOWARD, COUNTESS OF SOMERSET
Attributed to William Larkin, *c.*1615

Sir Thomas Overbury died, and is buried in the Tower. The manner of his death is not known, for that there was nobody with him, not so much as his Keeper. But the foulness of his corpse gave suspicion ... that he should die of the pox, or somewhat worse. He was a very unfortunate man, for nobody almost praises him, and his very friends speak but indifferently of him.

(John Chamberlain, 14 October 1613)

ROBERT CARR, EARL OF SOMERSET
Unknown artist, c.1611

Much about the case remains mysterious: the Carrs were convicted of the murder but were pardoned; four lesser accomplices – including the colourful, cunning woman and court madame, Anne Turner – were executed in 1615.

Overbury's poem about marriage, 'A Wife', was popular in its day. (This was published posthumously, with typical publisher's delicacy, as 'A Wife Now the Widow of Sir Thomas Overburie'.) According to Ben Jonson, Overbury was in love with the Countess of Rutland, the daughter of Sir Philip Sidney:

Overbury ... caused Ben to read his 'Wife' to her, which he [Jonson] with an excellent grace did, and praised the author. The morn thereafter he discorded with Overbury, who would have him to intend a suit that was unlawful.

Overbury's best-known work, generally known as 'Characters', is a series of pithy, topical vignettes such as 'A Roaring Boy' and 'A Mere Scholar'. This first appeared in 1614, appended to the second edition of 'A Wife'. Renold Elstrack's engraving of Overbury, which depicts him writing *His Epitaph written by himselfe*, was probably engraved and first published during 1615, the year when suspicions that Overbury had been poisoned were publicly raised.

Sir Henry Wotton (1568–1639)

W otton was a diplomat and dilettante whose main claim to literary fame is the miscellany of poems, essays and 'table-talk' collected under the title *Reliquiae Wottonianae* (1651).

Educated at Winchester and Oxford, he entered the service of the Earl of Essex in 1595. As Essex's secretary and intelligence-gatherer he was a rival of Anthony Bacon, brother of Francis. Though he was not implicated in the Essex Rising of 1601, he left the country to avoid recriminations. In 1602 he travelled incognito from Florence to Scotland, under the alias of 'Octavio Baldi', to warn King James of a Catholic plot to poison him. He was knighted by James in 1603, and the following year became ambassador to Venice.

> At his first going ambassador into Italy, as he passed through Germany, he [wrote] a pleasant definition of an ambassador, in these very words:
> 'Legatus est vir bonus peregre missus ad mentiendum Reipublicae causa'. Which Sir Henry Wotton could have been content should have been thus Englished: 'An ambassador is an honest man sent to lie abroad for the good of his country.'
>
> (Izaak Walton, Life of Wotton, 1651)

Wotton held various diplomatic appointments until his retirement in 1624. He then became provost of Eton, a post he held until his death. He published *The Elements of Architecture* (1624), of which the gossip John Chamberlain said: 'it is well-spoken of, though his own castles have been in the air'.

Wotton never married. Among his close friends were John Donne and Francis Bacon. Donne wrote to him praising the wandering life and freedom from the 'hell' of routine: 'Be thou thine own home, and in thy self dwell;/ Inn anywhere – continuance maketh hell'. Wotton shared with Izaak Walton a passion for fishing; the two men fished together at a stretch of the Thames near Eton called 'Black Pots'. Wotton wrote an account of the sport which predates Walton's *Compleat Angler*. His best-known poem is 'The Character of a Happy Life', which Ben Jonson said in 1619 he 'hath by heart'.

The wonderfully engaging portrait opposite is an old copy of the portrait at Eton, which was painted in the 1630s. It shows Wotton in

SIR HENRY WOTTON
Unknown artist

quizzically scholastic mode. The eyes watch us expectantly, the mouth has a thin smile of encouragement: we are almost audibly invited to debate, to challenge, or at least to amuse. The inscription besides him reads: *PHILOSOPHEMUR* – 'let us philosophise'.

EDWARD DE VERE, 17TH EARL OF OXFORD
Unknown artist

EDWARD DE VERE,
17TH EARL OF OXFORD (1550–1604)

Though claimed by some to be the author of Shakespeare's plays, in fact Oxford's literary output was aristocratically slight. Some fifteen poems are definitely his: clever, melodious and shallow. His life has an air of squandered brilliance.

Like the Howards and the Percys, the de Veres were aristocratic Catholics. Orphaned young, Edward was brought up by Lord Burghley. In 1567 he killed one of Burghley's servants, but was acquitted on a plea of self-defence. At the age of twenty-five, Oxford set off on a long and hugely expensive Grand Tour. This portrait shows him as he would have looked at this time, sumptuously decked out in shades of moleskin-grey and tangerine-red. He is haughty, fastidious, and faintly repellent.

In just over a year he spent £5000 (the equivalent of about £2 million nowadays) and 'lived in Florence in more grandeur than the Duke of Tuscany.' (John Aubrey) After his return to England, he became a by-word for fashionable Italianate affectations. In 1579, the Cambridge don Gabriel Harvey tilted at him in a satire, 'Speculum Tuscanismi'. This was reported to Oxford by his secretary, the author John Lyly, an enemy of Harvey's.

Rich and clever, Oxford seemed – especially after his marriage to Burghley's daughter – destined for high office but his temperament was unstable and capricious. In 1579 he quarrelled violently with Sir Philip Sidney during a tennis game – he called Sidney 'puppy' and threatened to kill him. He was deeply jealous of Ralegh, as Francis Bacon recalled.

In 1580 Oxford deserted his wife and daughter, when his affair with courtly acolyte Anne Vavasour bore a child. In the same year the Earl of Arundel affirmed: 'I will prove him a buggerer of a boy that is his cook'. Oxford was also accused of wild atheistic rants, such as calling the Virgin Mary a whore.

Little is known about the portrait illustrated here, which is on loan to the National Portrait Gallery from a private collection. The inscriptions indicate that the portrait represents Oxford at the age of twenty-five. It is thought to be a posthumous copy of a lost original painted during his lifetime.

Æ TATIS SVÆ 34
AN 1588

AMOR ET VIRTUTE.

SIR WALTER RALEGH
Attributed to the monogrammist 'H', 1588

SIR WALTER RALEGH (?1554–1618)

Ralegh was a high-achiever in so many walks of Elizabethan life – courtier, soldier, philosopher, historian, scientist, parliamentarian, explorer – that his brilliance as a poet is sometimes forgotten. He was born in Devon, and 'spake broad Devonshire to his dying day'. (John Aubrey) The Queen's nickname for him, 'Water', is Walter in a cod yokel accent.

The younger son of a moderately prosperous squire, Ralegh had to make his own way. He was the Elizabethan self-made man *par excellence.* The most famous piece of Ralegh folklore – the laying of his cloak in the mud for the Queen – encapsulates this. Unlike some other Ralegh legends (that he introduced tobacco to England, for instance) the cloak story has a surprising streak of authenticity. In its first guise it reads as follows:

> *This Captain Ralegh, coming out of Ireland to the English court in good habit (his clothes being then a considerable part of his estate) found the Queen walking, till meeting with a plashy place, she seemed to scruple going thereon. Presently Ralegh cast and spread his new plush cloak on the ground, whereon the Queen trod gently, rewarding him afterwards with many suits, for his so free and seasonable tender of so fair a footcloth.*

(Thomas Fuller, The Worthies of England, 1660)

This account is not quite contemporary, but there are documents that tend to corroborate it, and Ralegh did indeed present himself at court, bearing Irish despatches, in December 1581 (when the ground would indeed have been 'plashy' underfoot). The point of the story is not that Ralegh was obsequious, as is sometimes thought, but that he was prepared to gamble – he did not have plush cloaks to spare: it was perhaps his *only* cloak which he hazarded, and which won him many 'suits' as a result.

In the 1580s Ralegh rose vertiginously through the courtly ranks: he was the Queen's personal confidant and amorous sparring-partner, though she cannily declined to give him any real political or even landed power-base. He was knighted on 1 January 1585. The brilliant Hilliard miniature, the first portrait of Ralegh, belongs to this time: dark sultry looks, pearls and lace in abundance, the court dandy epitomised.

Ralegh was also at this time styled 'Lord and Governor of Virginia' – the English colony on the North American coast which he 'planted' and sponsored, but which he never actually visited. (This is another Ralegh

SIR WALTER RALEGH
Nicholas Hilliard, *c.*1585

legend: in fact the only bit of the Americas he visited was Venezuela, in 1595, in search of the ever-elusive 'golden city' of El Dorado.)

In the 1588 portrait, attributed to the monogrammist 'H', we see a plush cloak on Ralegh's shoulder, and a magnificent pearl earring (said to have been brought back from Virginia), and the motto which names his twin ideals as 'love and virtue'.

'Self-made' in the context of the Elizabethan court also implied being created by the Queen, and Ralegh fell spectacularly from favour in 1592, when his secret affair with one of the Queen's maids of honour, Elizabeth Throckmorton, was revealed; their son, Damerei, was born in March. After a brief spell in the Tower, the erring couple retired in disgrace to Ralegh's estate, Sherborne Castle, Dorset.

> *Sir Walter Ralegh was one that it seems Fortune had picked out of purpose, of whom to make an example or to use as her tennis ball … for she tossed him up of nothing, and to and fro, and from thence down to little more than that wherein she found him, a bare gentleman.*
>
> (Sir Robert Naunton, Fragmenta Regalia,1631)

Sir Walter Ralegh
Unknown artist, 1602

In 1593 Ralegh began work converting a Tudor hunting-lodge at Sherborne into the fine mansion which, with a few later additions, one sees today. For the next ten years he lived here: a country squire's life interspersed with adventures geographic and military, including the Guiana Voyage of 1595, the Azores Voyage of 1597 (with John Donne among the company), and the action at Cadiz. He was also a vigorous speaker in Parliament.

Ralegh was a compelling but curtailed figure during the last years of Elizabeth: he regained some power but not her full confidence. The full-length portrait of him and his second son, Wat, is dated 1602. He wears a white silk doublet and a pearl embroidered jacket, but the allure of the portrait lies in its quiet dignity, its sense of Ralegh's personal strength amid disappointments, and the poignant optimism of the young boy beside him. Wat (who was for a while tutored by Ben Jonson, and was to die on Ralegh's last voyage to South America, in 1618) is eight years old here.

In 1603 Sir Walter Ralegh's star fell once more. Embroiled in conspiracy against the new King James, he was despatched to the Tower under sentence of death. He remained there thirteen years, writing his *History of the World*, brewing his alchemical distillations in a converted henhouse in the Tower gardens, and petitioning for a last chance to find the fabled gold of Guiana. His wish was granted in 1617, but the expedition was a disaster, resulting in the suicide of his faithful servant Laurence Keymis and the death of Wat. The old treason charge was revived, and Ralegh was executed in Old Palace Yard, Westminster, in September 1618. His head was placed in a red velvet bag, and was kept by his widow until her death in the 1630s. It is said to lie in a vault in a Surrey church, where his youngest son Carew was buried.

Sir Francis Bacon (1561–1626)

A century after Bacon's death, the poet Pope summed him up as 'the wisest, brightest, meanest of mankind'. Of his brilliance there is no doubt – the range of his intellectual concerns, the toughness and lucidity of his prose, his tireless empiricism in an age still prone to what he called 'phantoms of the mind'. As Pope implied, however, Bacon's personality also contained an element of coldness and ruthlessness, and charges of personal treachery and corruption were levelled at him.

His best-known works are the *Essays* (1597), *The Advancement of Learning* (1605) and the *Novum Organum* (1620), but his name is more often evoked in the parlour-game context of his supposed authorship of Shakespeare's plays.

Bacon was the son of the corpulent and powerful politician, Sir Nicholas Bacon, and the uncle of the painter Nathaniel Bacon. His elder brother Anthony was also gifted, but dissipated his talents in intrigue and espionage, and died young of gout. In the 1590s Bacon was closely identified with the Earl of Essex's faction, but in 1601 he was chief prosecutor against the Earl after the latter's abortive 'rising' or coup. This episode is generally painted as a cynical performance, but he took part with some reluctance, under heavy pressure from the Queen, and when the inevitable verdict came he was active in urging clemency for Essex.

'Every honest man that hath his heart well planted,' he told the conspirator Mountjoy, 'will forsake his friend rather than forsake his King.' This was hardly a noble sentiment, but it suggests the dilemmas of his situation. Bacon was also involved in the trial and execution of Sir Walter Ralegh in 1618, and, as with Essex, has been cast as the heartless prosecutor of Ralegh at his most tragic and charismatic.

Bacon's star rose under King James – he became Solicitor General (1607), Attorney General (1613), Lord Keeper (1617) and Lord Chancellor (1618). In 1621, a hostile Parliament charged him with corruption: specifically, taking bribes in return for favourable judgments. He admitted guilt, accepted disgrace, and retired to his estate at Gorhambury, near St Albans. There he indulged his passion for gardening and wrote his strange last works, the *Sylva Sylvarum* and the *New Atlantis*, both published in 1627, a year after his death.

SIR FRANCIS BACON, unknown artist, after 1731

Bacon and his brother Anthony were homosexual. Anthony was actually charged with sodomy in France in the 1580s. In 1593 Bacon's mother complained of his intimacy with his servant Harry Percy, a 'proud, profane, costly fellow' who was his 'coach companion and bed companion'. Later in the seventeenth century, when Francis was vilified as a Stuart lackey, Sir Symonds d'Ewes spoke of his 'horrible and secret sin of sodomy', while Aubrey asserts that he was a 'paiderastes' surrounded by 'ganimedes'.

Bacon's marriage to Alice Barnham at the age of forty-six – very late by seventeenth-century standards – was marked by coldness and disharmony. He rewrote his will, revoking bequests to her, shortly before his death. Two weeks after he was buried, his teenage widow married a member of his staff, John Underhill. Aubrey adds that she made Underhill 'deaf and blind with too much Venus', implying a shortage of 'Venus' in the Baconian bed.

SIR FRANCIS BACON
Electrotype copy of marble tomb
effigy in St Michael's, St Albans

Bacon was described as of 'middling stature' and 'presence grave and comely'. The illustrated portrait, a later copy of the one at Gorhambury, shows Bacon in Chancellor's robes: the original must therefore have been painted in or after 1618. He was then in his mid-fifties, so the portrait hardly bears out Arthur Wilson's comment that 'his countenance had indented with age before he was old.' (*History of Great Britain*, 1653) In the portrait Bacon has brown hair and brown eyes, a characteristic tall black hat, and that shrewd, sceptical look which makes one think of his *Essays* – 'What is truth, said jesting Pilate, and would not stay for an answer'.

The marble tomb effigy in St Michael's church, St Albans, illustrated here by the electrotype copy in the National Portrait Gallery's collection, is unusual amongst the iconography of Elizabethan and Jacobean tomb effigies for its sense of world-weariness, even effeteness, and its contemplative mood seems appropriate to Bacon's 'presence grave'.

WRITERS AND THEIR PATRONS
❧

Patronage was an accepted fact of the Elizabethan literary world. The relationship varied: a patron might be the writer's friend, or his employer (the writer working as secretary or tutor, for example), or just the giver of occasional 'liberalities' and 'doles' which kept the wolf from the door. At its most functional, the patron simply paid a 'dedication fee' – typically £2 – in return for a slavish encomium at the beginning of a book. The theatrical companies also depended on patronage: they wore their patron's livery, and performed under his or her nominal protection.

The patronage system may seem archaic and demeaning today, and some writers resented the servitude – Nashe speaks bitterly of penning 'toys for private gentlemen', and of the wasted hours hanging around in the ante-chambers of 'Lord What-call-ye-him' – but it remains true that the glories of Elizabethan literature were made possible by the generosity and encouragement of a few rich and influential figures.

HENRY WRIOTHESLEY, 3RD EARL OF SOUTHAMPTON (1573–1624)

Southampton is probably the best-known of Elizabethan patrons due to his close association with Shakespeare, who dedicated *Venus and Adonis* (1593) and *The Rape of Lucrece* (1594) to him. The tone of the first dedication is formulaic, the second more personal – 'What I have done is yours, what I have to do is yours, being part in all I have, devoted yours'.

Southampton was then twenty years old, a wayward young aristocrat with wavering Catholic sympathies. He was also a very eligible bachelor whom Lord Burghley, his guardian, was keen to marry off to Elizabeth de Vere, the daughter of the Earl of Oxford. This may tie in with the opening sequence of Shakespeare's *Sonnets*, which is on the theme of marriage. It is certainly a good guess, if no more, that Southampton is the 'fair youth' addressed in the *Sonnets*, and that the relationship between patron and poet was close.

The Earl's striking, almost feline, looks and his flowing auburn hair (worn much longer than fashion dictated) are displayed in the fine full-length portrait illustrated here, on loan to the National Portrait Gallery from a private collection, and dated by costume to 1595–1600.

HENRY WRIOTHESLEY, 3RD EARL OF SOUTHAMPTON, unknown artist, *c*.1600

HENRY WRIOTHESLEY, 3RD EARL OF SOUTHAMPTON
After Daniel Mytens, *c.*1618?

(The helmet and breastplate might suggest a date around 1596, when Southampton took part in the naval assault on Cadiz.)

At Cadiz, and in much else, Southampton was a follower of the Earl of Essex, and he was deeply implicated in the Essex Rising of 1601. His death sentence was commuted to life-imprisonment, but he had served less than two years when the new King James released him and reinstated his earldom. His later life was morally upright: he was active in colonial ventures, becoming Treasurer of the Virginia Company in 1620, and he fought in the Netherlands, where he died of a fever, at Bergen-op-Zoom, in 1624. The later portrait, based on a painting by Daniel Mytens of *c.*1618, shows the Earl in his mid-forties, with a life of vicissitudes etched on the world-weary features.

Sir George Carey, 2nd Lord Hunsdon (1547–1603)

Sir George Carey was nominated Lord Chamberlain in 1597, and thus became the patron of Shakespeare's theatre company, the Lord Chamberlain's Men. The troupe had been formed three years earlier under the patronage of his father, Henry, 1st Lord Hunsdon. (This elder Hunsdon had a half-Italian mistress, Emilia Bassano, who is thought by some to be the 'Dark Lady' of Shakespeare's *Sonnets*.) The Lord Chamberlain's Men was the leading troupe of the day, with Richard Burbage its star actor and Will Kemp as resident comic. The first performance of *The Merry Wives of Windsor* was probably given in Carey's honour, when he was invested with the Order of the Garter, at Windsor, in March 1597.

Carey was a generous patron who, in the words of George Chapman, gave 'vital warmth to freezing science'. Thomas Nashe, in trouble with the

Sir George Carey
Nicholas Hilliard, 1601

London authorities in 1593 for satire in *Christ's Tears*, found shelter as his guest at Carisbrooke Castle in the Isle of Wight (Carey was governor of the island), and later said of him:

> *Whatsoever minute's intermission I have of calmed content proceedeth from him. Through him my tender wainscot study door is delivered from much assault and battery. Through him I look into and am looked on in the world, from whence otherwise I were a wretched banished exile.*

(Terrors of the Night, 1594)

Carey was also a patron of the composer John Dowland, who dedicated his *First Book of Songs and Airs* (1597) to him, and of the astrologer Simon Forman. The miniature by Hilliard shows him at the age of fifty-four, two years before his death from syphilis in 1603.

FERDINANDO STANLEY, 5TH EARL OF DERBY (*c.*1558–94)

This talented and popular nobleman was known as Lord Strange until his accession to the earldom on the death of his father in 1593. His theatre troupe, Strange's Men, was the leading company of the early 1590s, and formed the nucleus of the Lord Chamberlain's Men. Strange's Men performed Shakespeare's *Henry VI* and Marlowe's *Jew of Malta* at the Rose theatre in 1592. Under arrest in the Netherlands, Marlowe stated he was 'very well-known' to Lord Strange; Thomas Kyd confirms this, but adds that Strange 'could not endure' Marlowe once 'he learned of his conditions' [i.e. as an atheist].

Strange's circle was scholarly and occultist – Shakespeare may have been satirising it when he referred to the 'school of night' in *Love's Labours Lost*. Strange is almost certainly the 'Lord S' for whom Thomas Nashe wrote his bawdy poem, 'The Choice of Valentines', popularly known as 'Nashe's Dildo'. Other writers who praised Strange are George Chapman and Edmund Spenser. (The latter was a kinsman of Strange's wife, Alice, *née* Spenser.) Strange was himself a poet who, in Spenser's words, 'could pipe with passing skill'; some of his poems appeared in the popular anthology *Belvedere* (1600).

FERDINANDO STANLEY, 5TH EARL OF DERBY
James Stow after S. Harding

From a Catholic-tending family, and blood-related to the Queen on both sides of his family, Strange was bedevilled by Catholic plotters trying to persuade him into the role of pretender to the throne. One such persuader, Richard Hesketh, was hanged in 1593. Six months later, Strange died in great pain, at his house in Lathom, Lancashire. He believed he was the victim of witchcraft, but the symptoms suggest poison.

List of Illustrations

❧